G000138375

easy cakes & biscuits

THE AUSTRALIAN
Women's Weekly

CONTENTS

cakes	4
easy cupcakes	24
biscuits	26
easy shortbreads	44
easy kids' biscuits	46
slices	48
easy one-bowl slices	70
frostings, icings & fillings	72
glossary	74
conversion chart	77
index	78

AUSTRALIAN CUP AND SPOON MEASUREMENTS ARE METRIC. A CONVERSION CHART APPEARS ON PAGE 77.

These appealing cakes and biscuits look impressive. But they are so quick and easy to make that even the busiest of us can keep the biscuit tin and freezer full of delightful homemade treats.

Pamela Clark

Food Director

CUT & KEEP BUTTERCAKE

prep + cook time 1 hour 30 minutes **serves** 10

125g (4 ounces) butter, softened
1 teaspoon vanilla extract
1¼ cups (275g) caster (superfine) sugar
3 eggs
1 cup (150g) plain (all-purpose) flour
½ cup (75g) self-raising flour
¼ teaspoon bicarbonate of soda
    (baking soda)
½ cup (125ml) milk

1 Preheat oven to 180°C/350°F. Grease deep
20cm (8-inch) round cake pan; line base with
baking paper.
2 Beat ingredients in medium bowl on low
speed with electric mixer until just combined.
Increase speed to medium; beat about
3 minutes or until mixture is smooth and
pale in colour.
3 Spread mixture into pan; bake about
1¼ hours. Stand cake in pan 5 minutes before
turning, top-side up, onto wire rack to cool.
Dust cake with sifted icing (confectioners')
sugar, if desired.
tip Store cake in an airtight container for up to two days.

CAKES

pineapple sultana cake

UPSIDE-DOWN PEAR AND PISTACHIO CAKE

prep + cook time **50 minutes** serves **8**

¼ cup (35g) coarsely chopped
    unsalted pistachios
1 cup (220g) firmly packed light brown sugar
1 large pear (330g), unpeeled, cored,
    sliced thinly
185g (6 ounces) butter, softened
3 eggs
¼ cup (35g) plain (all-purpose) flour
1¾ cups (210g) ground almonds

1 Preheat oven to 200°C/400°F. Grease
shallow 22cm (9-inch) round cake pan; line
base with baking paper.
2 Combine nuts and 2 tablespoons of the
sugar in small bowl; sprinkle over base of pan,
top with pear slices.
3 Beat butter and remaining sugar in small
bowl with electric mixer until light and fluffy.
Beat in eggs, one at a time. Stir in sifted flour
and ground almonds.
4 Pour mixture into pan; bake about
35 minutes. Stand cake in pan 10 minutes
before turning, top-side down, onto wire rack.
Serve cake warm or cold.

tip Store cake in an airtight container for up to three days.

PINEAPPLE SULTANA CAKE

prep + cook time **1 hour 10 minutes (+ cooling)** serves **8**

440g (14 ounces) canned crushed
    pineapple in juice, drained
1 cup (150g) self-raising flour
½ cup (110g) caster (superfine) sugar
1 cup (80g) desiccated coconut
1 cup (160g) sultanas
1 egg, beaten lightly
½ cup (125ml) milk

1 Preheat oven to 180°C/350°F. Grease
14cm x 21cm (5½-inch x 8½-inch) loaf pan;
line base with baking paper, extending paper
5cm (2 inches) above long sides of pan.
2 Combine ingredients in large bowl. Pour
mixture into pan; bake about 50 minutes.
Stand loaf in pan 10 minutes before turning,
top-side up, onto wire rack to cool.

tip Store cake in an airtight container for up to four days.

upside-down pear and pistachio cake

ALMOND CARROT CAKE

prep + cook time **1 hour 35 minutes** serves **10**

5 eggs, separated
1 teaspoon finely grated lemon rind
1¼ cups (275g) caster (superfine) sugar
2 cups (480g) coarsely grated carrot
2 cups (240g) ground almonds
½ cup (75g) self-raising flour
2 tablespoons toasted slivered almonds
cream cheese frosting
100g (3 ounces) cream cheese, softened
80g (2½ ounces) butter, softened
½ cup (80g) icing (confectioners') sugar
1 teaspoon lemon juice

1 Preheat oven to 180°C/350°F. Grease deep 20cm (8-inch) square cake pan; line base with baking paper.
2 Beat egg yolks, rind and sugar in small bowl with electric mixer until thick and creamy; transfer to large bowl. Stir in carrot, ground almonds and sifted flour.
3 Beat egg whites in small bowl with electric mixer until soft peaks form; fold into carrot mixture, in two batches.
4 Pour mixture into pan; bake about 1¼ hours. Stand cake 5 minutes before turning, top-side up, onto wire rack to cool.
5 Meanwhile, make cream cheese frosting.
6 Spread cold cake with cream cheese frosting; sprinkle with slivered almonds.
cream cheese frosting Beat cream cheese and butter in small bowl with electric mixer until light and fluffy; gradually beat in sifted icing sugar and juice.

tips Store iced cake in an airtight container, in the fridge, for up to four days.

Both the carrot and the almond are thought to have come from North Africa and they have a flavour affinity that suits their being combined, both in savoury dishes and in baking. And there may be no sweeter example of this than this easy-to-make and good-keeping cake.

PRUNE AND CHOC-CHIP CAKE

prep + cook time **1 hour 15 minutes** serves **8**

1¼ cups (210g) seeded prunes
1¼ cups (310ml) boiling water
1 teaspoon bicarbonate of soda
   (baking soda)
60g (2 ounces) butter, chopped
¾ cup (165g) firmly packed light brown sugar
1 cup (160g) wholemeal self-raising flour
2 eggs
½ cup (95g) milk choc bits

1 Preheat oven to 180°C/350°F. Grease deep 20cm (8-inch) round cake pan; line base with baking paper.
2 Process prunes, the water and soda until combined; stand, covered, 5 minutes.
3 Add butter and sugar to processor; pulse until ingredients are combined. Add flour and eggs; pulse until combined. Stir in choc bits; pour mixture into pan.
4 Bake about 1 hour. Stand cake 5 minutes before turning, top-side up, onto wire rack to cool. Dust with sifted icing (confectioners') sugar, if you like.

tip **Store cake in an airtight container for up to a week.**

almond butter cake

ECONOMICAL BOILED FRUIT CAKE

prep + cook time **1 hour 45 minutes** serves **12**

2¾ cups (500g) mixed dried fruit
½ cup (125ml) water
1 cup (220g) firmly packed light brown sugar
125g (4 ounces) butter, chopped
1 teaspoon mixed spice
½ teaspoon bicarbonate of soda
    (baking soda)
½ cup (125ml) sweet sherry
1 egg
1 cup (150g) plain (all-purpose) flour
1 cup (150g) self-raising flour
⅓ cup (55g) blanched almonds
2 tablespoons sweet sherry, extra

1 Combine fruit, the water, sugar, butter, spice and soda in large saucepan. Stir over low heat, without boiling, until sugar dissolves and butter melts; bring to the boil. Reduce heat; simmer, covered, 5 minutes. Remove from heat; stir in sherry. Cool to room temperature.
2 Preheat oven to 160°C/325°F. Grease deep 20cm (8-inch) round cake pan; line base and side with two layers of baking paper, extending paper 5cm (2 inches) above side.
3 Stir egg and sifted flours into fruit mixture. Spread mixture into pan; decorate with almonds. Bake about 1½ hours. Brush top of hot cake with extra sherry. Cover cake with foil, cool in pan.

tip **Store cake in an airtight container for up to one month.**

ALMOND BUTTER CAKE

prep + cook time **1 hour 20 minutes** serves **10**

250g (8 ounces) butter, softened
1 teaspoon almond extract
1 cup (220g) caster (superfine) sugar
4 eggs
1 cup (150g) self-raising flour
½ cup (75g) plain (all-purpose) flour
¾ cup (90g) ground almonds

1 Preheat oven to 180°C/350°F. Grease deep 20cm (8-inch) square cake pan; line base and two opposite sides with baking paper, extending paper 5cm (2 inches) over edges.
2 Beat butter, extract and sugar in medium bowl with electric mixer until light and fluffy. Beat in eggs, one at a time. Fold in sifted flours and ground almonds, in two batches.
3 Spread mixture into pan; bake for 30 minutes. Reduce oven to 160°C/325°F; bake a further 30 minutes. Stand cake in pan 5 minutes before turning, top-side up, onto wire rack to cool. Serve dusted with sifted icing (confectioners') sugar and toasted flaked almonds, if you like.

tip **Store cake in an airtight container for up to two days.**

economical boiled fruit cake

quick-mix chocolate cake

QUICK-MIX CHOCOLATE CAKE

prep + cook time **1 hour 10 minutes** serves **10**

125g (4 ounces) butter, softened
1 teaspoon vanilla extract
1¼ cups (275g) caster (superfine) sugar
2 eggs
1⅓ cups (200g) self-raising flour
½ cup (50g) cocoa powder
⅔ cup (160ml) water
chocolate icing
90g (3 ounces) dark eating (semi-sweet)
  chocolate, chopped coarsely
30g (1 ounce) butter
1 cup (160g) icing (confectioners') sugar
2 tablespoons hot water

1 Preheat oven to 180°C/350°F. Grease
deep 20cm (8-inch) round cake pan; line
with baking paper.
2 Beat butter, extract, sugar, eggs, sifted flour
and cocoa and the water in large bowl with
electric mixer on low speed until ingredients
are combined. Increase speed to medium;
beat about 3 minutes or until mixture is
smooth and paler in colour.
3 Spread mixture into pan; bake about 1 hour.
Stand cake in pan 5 minutes before turning,
top-side up, onto wire rack to cool.
4 Meanwhile, make chocolate icing. Spread
cold cake with icing.
chocolate icing Melt chocolate and butter in
small heatproof bowl over small saucepan of
simmering water; gradually stir in sifted icing
sugar and the hot water, stirring until icing is
spreadable.
tip **store cake in an airtight container for up to
three days.**

pound cake

POUND CAKE

prep + cook time **1 hour 20 minutes** serves **12**

250g (8 ounces) butter, softened
1 cup (220g) caster (superfine) sugar
1 teaspoon vanilla extract
4 eggs
½ cup (75g) self-raising flour
1 cup (150g) plain (all-purpose) flour

1 Preheat oven to 180°C/350°F. Grease deep
20cm (8-inch) round cake pan; line base with
baking paper.
2 Beat butter, sugar and extract in small bowl
with electric mixer until light and fluffy. Beat in
eggs, one at a time. Transfer mixture to large
bowl; fold in sifted flours, in two batches.
3 Spread mixture into pan; bake about 1 hour.
Stand cake in pan 5 minutes before turning,
top-side up, onto wire rack to cool. If you like,
serve with whipped cream and strawberries,
and dust with sifted icing (confectioners') sugar.
tip **Store cake in an airtight container for up to three
days.**

CHOCOLATE BANANA CAKE

prep + cook time **1 hour 30 minutes** serves **10**

⅔ cup (160ml) milk
2 teaspoons lemon juice
150g (4½ ounces) butter, softened
1 cup (220g) caster (superfine) sugar
2 eggs
2 cups (300g) self-raising flour
½ teaspoon bicarbonate of soda
    (baking soda)
1 cup mashed banana
100g (3 ounces) dark eating (semi-sweet)
    chocolate, grated finely
creamy choc frosting
200g (6½ ounces) dark eating
    (semi-sweet) chocolate
1 cup (160g) icing (confectioners') sugar
½ cup (120g) sour cream

1 Preheat oven to 170°C/340°F. Grease deep 22cm (9-inch) round cake pan; line base with paper.
2 Combine milk and juice in small jug; stand 10 minutes.
3 Meanwhile, beat butter and sugar in small bowl with electric mixer until light and fluffy. Beat in eggs, one at a time; transfer mixture to large bowl. Stir in sifted flour and soda, banana, milk mixture and chocolate.
4 Spread mixture into pan; bake about 1 hour 10 minutes. Stand cake 5 minutes before turning, top-side up, onto wire rack to cool.
5 Meanwhile, make creamy choc frosting. Spread cold cake with frosting.

creamy choc frosting Melt chocolate in medium heatproof bowl over medium saucepan of simmering water; gradually stir in sifted icing sugar and sour cream.

tips Store iced cake in an airtight container, in the fridge, for up to three days.

You will need approximately 2 large overripe bananas (460g) for this recipe. It is very important that the bananas you use are overripe; less-ripe ones won't mash easily and can cause the cake to be too heavy. A banana's natural starch is converted to sugar during the ripening process, and it's this natural sugar that contributes to the correct balance of ingredients. The cake also develops quite a thick crust because of this sugar content.

pineapple coconut cake

PINEAPPLE COCONUT CAKE

prep + cook time **1 hour** serves **20**

185g (6 ounces) butter, softened
¾ cup (165g) caster (superfine) sugar
3 eggs
⅔ cup (50g) desiccated coconut
1¾ cups (260g) self-raising flour
1 cup (250ml) canned coconut cream
440g (14 ounces) canned crushed
　　pineapple, well-drained
⅓ cup (25g) shredded coconut
lime glacé icing
1½ cups (240g) icing (confectioners') sugar
20g (¾ ounce) butter, melted
2 tablespoons lime juice, approximately

1 Preheat oven to 180°C/350°F. Grease
22cm x 32cm (9-inch x 13-inch) rectangular
cake pan; line base and sides with baking paper,
extending paper 5cm (2 inches) over edges.
2 Beat butter and sugar in small bowl with
electric mixer until light and fluffy. Beat in eggs,
one at a time. Transfer mixture to large bowl;
stir in coconut, sifted flour, coconut cream and
pineapple, in two batches.
3 Spread mixture into pan; bake about
45 minutes. Stand cake in pan 10 minutes
before turning, top-side up, onto wire rack
to cool.
4 Meanwhile, make lime glacé icing; spread
icing over cake, sprinkle with coconut.
lime glacé icing Sift icing sugar into small
heatproof bowl; stir in butter and enough
of the juice to make a soft paste. Stir over
small saucepan of simmering water until icing
is spreadable.
tip **Store cake in an airtight container for up to
three days.**

one-bowl sultana loaf

ONE-BOWL SULTANA LOAF

prep + cook time **1 hour 45 minutes** serves **8**

125g (4 ounces) butter, melted
750g (1½ pounds) sultanas
½ cup (110g) firmly packed light brown sugar
2 tablespoons marmalade
2 eggs, beaten lightly
¼ cup (60ml) sweet sherry
¾ cup (110g) plain (all-purpose) flour
¼ cup (35g) self-raising flour
¼ cup (40g) blanched almonds
2 tablespoons apricot jam

1 Preheat oven to 150°C/300°F. Grease
15cm x 25cm (6-inch x 10-inch) loaf pan;
line base with baking paper.
2 Beat butter, sultanas, sugar, marmalade,
egg, sherry and flours in large bowl using a
wooden spoon until combined.
3 Spread mixture into pan; decorate top with
blanched almonds. Bake about 1½ hours.
Cover cake with foil; cool in pan. Brush cold
cake with warmed sieved apricot jam.
tip **Store loaf in an airtight container for up to a week.**

CHOCOLATE FUDGE CAKE

prep + cook time **50 minutes** serves **12**

250g (8 ounces) dark eating (semi-sweet)
  chocolate, chopped
125g (4 ounces) butter, chopped coarsely
⅔ cup (150g) caster (superfine) sugar
⅔ cup (100g) self-raising flour
4 eggs, beaten lightly

1 Preheat oven to 180°C/350°F. Grease
20cm x 30cm (8-inch x 12-inch) rectangular
pan; line base and long sides with baking
paper, extending paper 5cm (2 inches)
over sides.
2 Stir chocolate and butter in medium
heatproof bowl over medium saucepan of
simmering water (do not allow the water to
touch base of bowl); cool.
3 Combine chocolate mixture and remaining
ingredients in medium bowl; beat on low speed
with electric mixer until ingredients are
combined. Increase speed to medium; beat
about 3 minutes or until mixture is changed in
colour and smooth.
4 Pour mixture into pan; bake about 30 minutes.
Stand cake in pan 5 minutes before turning,
top-side up, onto wire rack to cool. Serve
dusted with sifted cocoa powder, if desired.
tip **Store cake in an airtight container for up to a week.**

orange cake

ORANGE CAKE

prep + cook time **50 minutes** serves **12**

150g (4½ ounces) butter, softened
1 tablespoon finely grated orange rind
⅔ cup (150g) caster (superfine) sugar
3 eggs
1½ cups (225g) self-raising flour
¼ cup (60ml) milk
¾ cup (120g) icing (confectioners') sugar
1½ tablespoons orange juice

1 Preheat oven to 180°C/350°F. Grease deep
20cm (8-inch) round cake pan.
2 Beat butter, rind, caster sugar, eggs, flour
and milk in medium bowl with electric mixer on
low speed until just combined. Increase speed
to medium; beat about 3 minutes or until
mixture is smooth.
3 Spread mixture into pan; bake about
40 minutes. Stand cake in pan 5 minutes before
turning, top-side up, onto wire rack to cool.
4 Combine sifted icing sugar and juice in small
bowl; spread over cake.
tip **Store cake in an airtight container for up to four days.**

chocolate fudge cake

MAPLE PECAN CAKE

prep + cook time **1 hour 15 minutes** serves **10**

cooking-oil spray
1 cup (100g) pecan nuts
⅓ cup (80ml) pure maple syrup
1¼ cups (310ml) boiling water
1¼ cups (235g) coarsely chopped dried figs
1 teaspoon bicarbonate of soda (baking soda)
60g (2 ounces) butter
¾ cup (150g) firmly packed light brown sugar
2 eggs
1 cup (150g) self-raising flour
maple butterscotch sauce
1 cup (250ml) pure maple syrup
½ cup (125ml) pouring cream
100g (3 ounces) butter, chopped coarsely

1 Preheat oven to 180°C/350°F. Grease deep 20cm (8-inch) round cake pan; line base with baking paper. Spray paper with oil.

2 Arrange nuts over base of pan; drizzle with maple syrup.

3 Combine the water, figs and soda in bowl of food processor. Cover with lid; stand 5 minutes. Add butter and sugar; process until almost smooth. Add eggs and flour; process until just combined.

4 Pour mixture into prepared pan; bake about 55 minutes. Stand cake in pan 5 minutes before turning onto wire rack. Serve warm cake with maple butterscotch sauce and, if desired, vanilla ice-cream.

maple butterscotch sauce Stir ingredients in small saucepan over heat until smooth; bring to the boil. Boil, uncovered, about 2 minutes or until mixture thickens slightly.

tip **Cake is best eaten the day it is made.**

Decorate any of your favourite cupcakes with these simple ideas. See page 72 for frosting and icing recipes. Cakes are best eaten on the day they are iced.

DAISY CAKES

Make butter cream; spread over cake tops. Cut marshmallows in half horizontally; squeeze the ends together to form petals. Decorate cakes with petals; position a smartie in the centre of each daisy.

SUGARED BERRY CAKES

Make butter cream; spread over cake tops. Brush fresh berries sparingly with lightly beaten egg white; gently roll the wet fruit in caster (superfine) sugar. Position on cakes.

EASY CUPCAKES

STRAWBERRY CREAM CAKES

Make butter cream; spread over cake tops.
Remove the green top from strawberries, slice
thinly and arrange on top of cakes to make
flowers. Brush with warmed, strained
strawberry jam.

CHOCOLATE CURL CAKES

Make dark chocolate ganache; spread over
cake tops. Spread melted dark chocolate onto
a cold surface; when set, drag a melon baller
over the chocolate to make curls. Arrange on
top of cakes.

CHUNKY CHOCOLATE-CHIP COOKIES

prep + cook time 30 minutes makes 36

125g (4 ounces) butter, softened
1 teaspoon vanilla extract
1¼ cups (275g) firmly packed light
    brown sugar
1 egg
1 cup (150g) plain (all-purpose) flour
¼ cup (35g) self-raising flour
½ teaspoon bicarbonate of soda
    (baking soda)
⅓ cup (35g) cocoa powder
½ cup (100g) peanut m&m's
⅓ cup (70g) mini m&m's
½ cup (75g) milk chocolate melts

1 Preheat oven to 180°C/350°F. Grease two oven trays; line with baking paper.
2 Beat butter, extract, sugar and egg in small bowl with electric mixer until smooth (do not overmix). Transfer mixture to large bowl; stir in sifted dry ingredients then all chocolates.
3 Drop level tablespoons of mixture about 5cm (2 inches) apart onto trays.
4 Bake about 10 minutes; stand cookies on trays 5 minutes before transferring to wire rack to cool.

tip Store cookies in an airtight container for up to three weeks. Freeze for up to three months.

BISCUITS

CHOCOLATE CHIP COOKIES

prep + cook time **30 minutes** makes **36**

250g (8 ounces) butter, softened
1 teaspoon vanilla extract
¾ cup (165g) caster (superfine) sugar
¾ cup (165g) firmly packed light brown sugar
1 egg
2¼ cups (335g) plain (all-purpose) flour
1 teaspoon bicarbonate of soda (baking soda)
375g (12 ounces) dark chocolate melts,
    chopped coarsely

1 Preheat oven to 180°C/350°F. Grease oven trays.
2 Beat butter, extract, sugars and egg in small bowl with electric mixer until light and fluffy. Transfer mixture to large bowl; stir in sifted flour and soda, in two batches. Stir in chocolate.
3 Roll tablespoons of mixture into balls, place about 5cm (2 inches) apart on trays; bake about 15 minutes. Cool on trays.

tips Store in an airtight container for up to a week. Dark chocolate can be replaced with milk or white chocolate. For choc-nut cookies, replace a third of the chocolate with roasted chopped nuts such as hazelnuts, walnuts, pecans or macadamias.

chewy chocolate caramel cookies

CHEWY CHOCOLATE CARAMEL COOKIES

prep + cook time **25 minutes** makes **24**

125g (4 ounces) butter, softened
½ cup (110g) caster (superfine) sugar
1 egg
1 cup (150g) plain (all-purpose) flour
2 tablespoons cocoa powder
120g (2 ounces) chokito bars,
    chopped finely

1 Preheat oven to 180°C/350°F. Grease oven trays; line with baking paper.
2 Beat butter, sugar and egg in small bowl with electric mixer until smooth; do not overbeat. Transfer mixture to medium bowl; stir in sifted flour and cocoa, then chopped chocolate bar.
3 Drop level tablespoons of mixture about 5cm (2 inches) apart onto trays; bake about 15 minutes. Cool on trays.

tip Store in an airtight container for up to a week. Chokito bars are chocolate-coated caramel fudge bars with crunchy rice crisps. They are available from supermarkets and confectionery stores.

chocolate chip cookies

spiced treacle cookies

SPICED TREACLE COOKIES

prep + cook time **35 minutes** makes **34**

75g (2½ ounces) butter, chopped coarsely
⅓ cup (120g) treacle
¼ cup (55g) firmly packed light brown sugar
¾ cup (110g) plain (all-purpose) flour
½ cup (75g) self-raising flour
1 teaspoon ground cinnamon
1 teaspoon mixed spice
¼ cup (30g) finely chopped walnuts
1 tablespoon light brown sugar, extra

1 Preheat oven to 160°C/325°F. Grease oven trays; line with baking paper.
2 Combine butter, treacle and sugar in medium saucepan; stir over low heat until smooth. Cool 5 minutes; stir in sifted flours and spices.
3 Roll rounded teaspoons of mixture into balls; place about 5cm (2 inches) apart on trays, flatten slightly. Sprinkle with combined nuts and extra sugar. Bake about 20 minutes; cool on trays.

tip **Store cookies in an airtight container for up to four days.**

coconut macaroons

COCONUT MACAROONS

prep + cook time **1 hour** makes **18**

1 egg, separated
1 egg yolk
¼ cup (55g) caster (superfine) sugar
1⅔ cups (125g) shredded coconut

1 Preheat oven to 150°C/300°F. Grease oven trays; line with baking paper.
2 Beat egg yolks and sugar in small bowl until creamy; stir in coconut.
3 Beat egg white in small bowl until firm peaks form; stir gently into coconut mixture. Drop heaped teaspoons of mixture onto trays.
4 Bake macaroons about 15 minutes.
5 Reduce oven to 120°C/250°F; bake further 30 minutes or until biscuits are golden brown. Loosen biscuits while warm; cool on trays.

tip **Store in an airtight container for up to three weeks. Freeze for up to three months.**

GOLDEN OATY CARROT BISCUITS

prep + cook time 35 minutes makes 44

125g (4 ounces) butter, softened
1 cup (220g) firmly packed light brown sugar
1 egg yolk
½ cup (70g) firmly packed coarsely
    grated carrot
1½ cups (225g) plain (all-purpose) flour
½ teaspoon bicarbonate of soda (baking soda)
1 teaspoon ground cinnamon
1 cup (90g) rolled oats
1 tablespoon milk, approximately

1 Preheat oven to 180°C/350°F. Line oven
trays with baking paper.
2 Beat butter, sugar and egg yolk in small bowl
with electric mixer until combined. Stir in carrot,
then sifted flour, soda and cinnamon. Stir in
oats and enough milk to make a firm dough.
3 Roll heaped teaspoons of mixture into balls;
place about 5cm (2 inches) apart on trays, flatten
slightly. Bake about 15 minutes; cool on trays.
tip Store biscuits in an airtight container for up to a week.

anzac biscuits

ANZAC BISCUITS

prep + cook time 35 minutes makes 25

125g (4 ounces) butter, chopped
2 tablespoons golden syrup or treacle
1 tablespoon water
½ teaspoon bicarbonate of soda (baking soda)
1 cup (220g) firmly packed light brown sugar
½ cup (40g) desiccated coconut
1 cup (90g) rolled oats
1 cup (150g) plain (all-purpose) flour

1 Preheat oven to 160°C/325°F. Line oven
trays with baking paper.
2 Stir butter, syrup and the water in large
saucepan over low heat until smooth. Remove
from heat; stir in soda then remaining ingredients.
3 Roll tablespoons of mixture into balls; place
about 5cm (2 inches) apart on trays, flatten
slightly. Bake about 20 minutes; cool on trays.
tips Store biscuits in an airtight container for up
to a week. Biscuits should still feel soft when they're
cooked; they will firm up as they cool.

traditional shortbread

TRADITIONAL SHORTBREAD

prep + cook time **1 hour** makes **24**

250g (8 ounces) butter, softened
⅓ cup (75g) caster (superfine) sugar
1 tablespoon water
2 cups (300g) plain (all-purpose) flour
½ cup (90g) rice flour
2 tablespoons white (granulated) sugar

1 Preheat oven to 160°C/325°F. Grease oven trays.
2 Beat butter and caster sugar in medium bowl with electric mixer until light and fluffy; stir in the water and sifted flours, in two batches. Knead mixture on floured surface until smooth.
3 Divide mixture in half; shape each half on separate trays into 20cm (8-inch) rounds. Mark each round into 12 wedges; prick with fork. Pinch edges of rounds with fingers; sprinkle shortbread with white sugar.
4 Bake about 40 minutes; stand 5 minutes. Using sharp knife, cut into wedges along marked lines. Cool on trays.

tips Store shortbread in an airtight container for up to a week. Ground white rice can be used instead of rice flour, although it is slightly coarser in texture.

cream cheese, coconut and lime cookies

CREAM CHEESE, COCONUT AND LIME COOKIES

prep + cook time **40 minutes** makes **36**

250g (8 ounces) butter, softened
90g (3 ounces) cream cheese, softened
1 tablespoon finely grated lime rind
1 cup (220g) firmly packed light brown sugar
2 eggs
1¼ cups (185g) plain (all-purpose) flour
1 cup (150g) self-raising flour
½ cup (40g) desiccated coconut

1 Preheat oven to 180°C/350°F. Grease oven trays; line with baking paper.
2 Beat butter, cream cheese, rind and sugar in small bowl with electric mixer until light and fluffy. Beat in eggs, one at a time. Transfer mixture to large bowl; stir in sifted flours and coconut, in two batches.
3 Roll level tablespoons of dough into balls; place about 5cm (2 inches) apart on trays, flatten slightly. Bake about 15 minutes; cool on trays.

tip Store cookies in an airtight container for up to a week.

almond crisps

ALMOND CRISPS

prep + cook time **35 minutes** makes **15**

125g (4 ounces) butter, softened
¼ cup (55g) caster (superfine) sugar
1 cup (150g) self-raising flour
¼ cup (30g) ground almonds
2 tablespoons flaked almonds

1 Preheat oven to 200°C/400°F. Grease oven trays; line with baking paper.
2 Beat butter and sugar in small bowl with electric mixer until smooth. Stir in sifted flour and ground almonds.
3 Roll level tablespoons of mixture into balls; place about 5cm (2 inches) apart onto trays. Flatten slightly with a floured fork to 1cm (½-inch) thick; sprinkle with flaked almonds.
4 Bake about 10 minutes; stand crisps on trays 5 minutes before transferring to wire racks to cool.

tip **Store crisps in an airtight container for up to two weeks.**

JAM DROPS

prep + cook time **40 minutes** makes **24**

125g (4 ounces) butter, softened
½ teaspoon vanilla extract
½ cup (110g) caster (superfine) sugar
1 cup (120g) ground almonds
1 egg
1 cup (150g) plain (all-purpose) flour
1 teaspoon finely grated lemon rind
⅓ cup (110g) raspberry jam
2 tablespoons apricot jam

1 Preheat oven to 180°C/350°F. Line oven trays with baking paper.
2 Beat butter, extract, sugar and ground almonds in small bowl with electric mixer until light and fluffy. Beat in egg; stir in sifted flour.
3 Divide rind between both jams; mix well.
4 Roll tablespoons of mixture into balls; place about 5cm (2 inches) apart on trays, flatten slightly. Using end of a wooden spoon, press a flower shape, about 1cm (½-inch) deep, into dough; fill each hole with a little jam, using raspberry jam for petals of flowers and apricot jam for centres.
5 Bake about 15 minutes; cool on trays.

tip **Store biscuits in an airtight container for up to two days.**

jam drops

CRUNCHY MUESLI COOKIES

prep + cook time **40 minutes** makes **36**

1 cup (90g) rolled oats
1 cup (150g) plain (all-purpose) flour
1 cup (220g) caster (superfine) sugar
2 teaspoons ground cinnamon
¼ cup (35g) dried cranberries
⅓ cup (55g) finely chopped dried apricots
½ cup (70g) slivered almonds
125g (4 ounces) butter
2 tablespoons golden syrup or treacle
½ teaspoon bicarbonate of soda (baking soda)
1 tablespoon boiling water

1 Preheat oven to 150°C/300°F. Grease oven trays; line with baking paper.
2 Combine oats, flour, sugar, cinnamon, dried fruit and nuts in large bowl.
3 Stir butter and golden syrup in small saucepan over low heat until smooth; stir in combined soda and the boiling water. Stir warm butter mixture into dry ingredients.
4 Roll level tablespoons of mixture into balls; place about 5cm (2 inches) apart on trays, flatten slightly. Bake about 20 minutes; cool on trays.

tip Store cookies in an airtight container for up to a week.

PECAN CHOC-CHUNK COOKIES

prep + cook time **30 minutes** makes **28**

125g (4 ounces) butter, softened
¼ cup (55g) caster (superfine) sugar
¼ cup (55g) firmly packed light brown sugar
1 egg
1 cup (150g) plain (all-purpose) flour
¾ cup (90g) ground pecans
150g (4½ ounces) milk eating chocolate,
    chopped coarsely
½ cup (60g) coarsely chopped pecans

1 Preheat oven to 180°C/350°F. Grease oven trays; line with baking paper.
2 Beat butter, sugars and egg in small bowl with electric mixer until combined; stir in sifted flour, ground pecans, chocolate and chopped pecans.
3 Drop level tablespoons of mixture about 5cm (2 inches) apart on trays; flatten slightly. Bake about 15 minutes; cool on trays.

tip **Store biscuits in an airtight container for up to a week. You will need approximately 1 cup (120g) pecans to make enough ground pecans for this recipe.**

CARAMEL PECAN MACAROONS

prep + cook time **55 minutes** makes **22**

1⅔ cups (200g) pecans
2 egg whites
½ cup (110g) firmly packed light brown sugar
1 teaspoon vanilla extract
¼ cup (35g) plain (all-purpose) flour
22 pecan halves

1 Preheat oven to 150°C/300°F. Grease oven trays; line with baking paper.
2 Blend or process pecans until ground finely.
3 Beat egg whites and sugar in small bowl with electric mixer about 15 minutes or until sugar is dissolved. Stir in extract, sifted flour and ground pecans, in two batches.
4 Drop rounded tablespoons of mixture 5cm (2 inches) apart onto trays. Press one nut half on top of each macaroon. Bake about 30 minutes; cool on trays.

tip **Store macaroons in an airtight container for up to a week.**

pecan choc-chunk cookies

macadamia shortbread

MACADAMIA SHORTBREAD

prep + cook time **40 minutes** makes **24**

250g (8 ounces) butter, softened, chopped
½ cup (110g) caster (superfine) sugar
2 teaspoons vanilla extract
2 cups (300g) plain (all-purpose) flour
½ cup (75g) rice flour
½ cup (75g) finely chopped macadamias
2 tablespoons caster (superfine) sugar, extra

1 Preheat oven to 160°C/325°F. Grease oven trays.
2 Beat butter, sugar and extract in small bowl with electric mixer until light and fluffy. Transfer mixture to large bowl; stir in sifted flours and nuts, in two batches. Knead on floured surface until smooth.
3 Divide mixture in half; shape each half into 25cm (10-inch) rounds. Press an upturned 24cm (9½-inch) loose-based fluted flan tin into shortbread to cut rounds. Cut each round into 12 wedges; place on trays, prick with fork. Sprinkle shortbread with extra sugar.
4 Bake about 20 minutes; stand 10 minutes before transferring to wire racks to cool.
tip Store shortbread in an airtight container for up to three weeks. Freeze for up to three months.

dutch ginger biscuits

DUTCH GINGER BISCUITS

prep + cook time **35 minutes** makes **36**

250g (8 ounces) butter, softened
¾ cup (165g) firmly packed light brown sugar
1 egg
2 cups (300g) plain (all-purpose) flour
1 teaspoon ground ginger
⅓ cup (60g) finely chopped glacé ginger

1 Preheat oven to 180°C/350°F. Grease oven trays; line with baking paper.
2 Beat butter, sugar and egg in small bowl with electric mixer until combined. Stir in sifted flour and ground ginger, in two batches. Stir in glacé ginger.
3 Roll level tablespoons of dough into balls; place about 5cm (2 inches) apart on trays, flatten with fork. Bake about 15 minutes; cool on trays.
tip Store biscuits in an airtight container for up to a week.

BASIC SHORTBREAD DOUGH

prep time **15 minutes** makes **1 quantity**

Beat 250g (8 ounces) softened butter, ¼ cup (55g) caster (superfine) sugar and 1 teaspoon vanilla extract in small bowl with electric mixer until smooth. Transfer to large bowl; stir in 1½ cups (225g) sifted plain (all-purpose) flour, in two batches.

LATTE SHORTBREAD DIPPERS

prep + cook time **40 minutes** makes **32**

Preheat oven to 160°C/325°F. Line oven trays with baking paper. Make 1 quantity basic shortbread dough (recipe left). Dissolve 1 tablespoon instant coffee granules in 1 teaspoon boiling water; stir coffee mixture into dough. Spoon mixture into piping bag fitted with a 2cm (¾-inch) fluted tube. Pipe 6cm (2¼-inch) lengths about 2.5cm (1 inch) apart onto trays; sprinkle with 1 tablespoon demerara or white (granulated) sugar. Bake about 15 minutes; cool on trays.

tip **Store shortbread dippers in an airtight container for up to a week.**

EASY SHORTBREADS

GINGER LIME SHORTBREADS

prep + cook time **50 minutes** makes **30**

Preheat oven to 160°C/325°F. Line oven
trays with baking paper. Make 1 quantity
basic shortbread dough (opposite page).
Stir in 2 teaspoons finely grated lime rind,
2 tablespoons finely chopped glacé ginger,
¾ cup (90g) ground almonds, 2 teaspoons
ground ginger and ¼ cup (35g) finely
chopped roasted unsalted cashews. Shape
level tablespoons of mixture into mounds
about 2.5cm (1 inch) apart on trays; top each
mound with a whole roasted unsalted cashew.
Bake about 25 minutes; cool on trays.

tip Store shortbread in an airtight container for up
to a week.

GOLDEN SYRUP PEANUT SWIRLS

prep + cook time **30 minutes** makes **60**

Preheat oven to 180°C/350°F. Line oven trays
with baking paper. Make 1 quantity basic
shortbread dough (opposite page) replacing
vanilla extract with 1 tablespoon golden syrup
or treacle. Stir ¼ cup (70g) smooth peanut
butter into dough. Spoon mixture into piping
bag fitted with a 2cm (¾-inch) fluted tube;
pipe 5cm (2-inch) stars about 2.5cm (1 inch)
apart onto trays. Bake about 10 minutes;
cool on trays.

tip Store swirls in an airtight container for up to a week.

We used plain oval biscuits, spread with royal icing (see recipe on page 73). Prepare decorations before spreading with icing, as the icing begins to set as soon as it is spread onto the biscuits. These biscuits are best eaten on the day they are iced.

FLOWERS

Cut fine slices of mint leaf lollies to make the leaves and stems. Ice the biscuits, position the stems and leaves immediately, then position ready-made icing flowers. The flowers can be found in the baking section of supermarkets.

HEARTS

Heart-shaped lollies can be bought from sweet shops. Position them on the icing before it sets. Use the hearts to outline various shapes, such as diamonds or stars, make numbers, or the initial of each guest.

EASY KIDS' BISCUITS

ROCKET MAN

The two top sections are shaped from pieces taken from disassembled licorice allsorts, we used an m&m on the top section. The feet are made from fruit allsorts. Assemble the rocket man on the biscuit before the icing sets.

RIBBONS & BOWS

We made the ribbons and bows by cutting very thin strips from red sour straps. Position the ribbons before the icing sets, secure the bows to the ribbons with a tiny dot of the icing.

CHOCOLATE FRECKLE SLICE

prep + cook time 45 minutes **makes** 35

185g (6 ounces) butter, softened
220g (7 ounces) chocolate hazelnut spread
⅓ cup (75g) firmly packed light brown sugar
1¾ cups (250g) plain (all-purpose) flour
200g (6½ ounces) freckles

1 Preheat oven to 160°C/325°F. Grease
20cm x 30cm (8-inch x 12-inch) rectangular
pan; line base and long sides with baking paper,
extending paper 5cm (2 inches) over sides.
2 Beat butter, spread and sugar in small bowl
with electric mixer until combined. Stir in sifted
flour, in two batches.
3 Press dough into pan; smooth surface with
spatula. Bake 25 minutes. Remove pan from
oven; working quickly, press freckles firmly onto
slice in rows about 2cm (¾ inch) apart. Cool
slice in pan before cutting.

tips Store slice in an airtight container for up to three
days. Freckles are small chocolate discs covered with
hundreds and thousands (nonpareils). They are
available from supermarkets and confectionery stores.

SLICES

tangy lemon squares

FLORENTINE SLICE

prep + cook time **25 minutes (+ refrigeration)** makes **24**

¾ cup (120g) sultanas
2 cups (80g) corn flakes
¾ cup (110g) unsalted peanuts
1 cup (175g) coarsely chopped milk
    eating chocolate
½ cup (100g) red glacé cherries, halved
395g (12½ ounces) canned sweetened
    condensed milk
¼ cup (60ml) ice magic chocolate topping

1 Preheat oven to 180°C/350°F. Grease
20cm x 30cm (8-inch x 12-inch) rectangular
pan; line base and long sides with baking
paper, extending paper 5cm (2 inches)
over sides.
2 Combine sultanas, corn flakes, nuts,
chocolate and cherries in pan; drizzle
condensed milk all over mixture.
3 Bake about 15 minutes or until browned
lightly; cool in pan. Drizzle slice with chocolate
topping; refrigerate until set. Cut into small
rectangles to serve.
tip Store slice in an airtight container for up to three days.

TANGY LEMON SQUARES

prep + cook time **55 minutes** makes **16**

125g (4 ounces) butter, softened
¼ cup (40g) icing (confectioners') sugar
1¼ cups (185g) plain (all-purpose) flour
3 eggs
1 cup (220g) caster (superfine) sugar
2 teaspoons finely grated lemon rind
½ cup (125ml) lemon juice

1 Preheat oven to 180°C/350°F. Grease 22cm
(9-inch) square slab pan; line base with baking
paper, extending paper 5cm (2 inches) over
two opposite sides.
2 Beat butter and icing sugar in small bowl
with electric mixer until smooth. Stir in 1 cup
(150g) of the flour. Press mixture over base of
pan. Bake base about 15 minutes or until
browned lightly.
3 Meanwhile, whisk eggs, caster sugar,
remaining flour, rind and juice in bowl until
combined; pour over hot base.
4 Bake slice further 20 minutes or until firm.
Cool slice in pan, on wire rack, before cutting.
Dust with extra sifted icing sugar, if you like.
tip Refrigerate in an airtight container for up to three days

florentine slice

triple chocolate slice

TRIPLE CHOCOLATE SLICE

prep + cook time **40 minutes (+ refrigeration)** makes **30**

250g (8 ounces) plain chocolate biscuits
325g (10½ ounces) dark eating (semi-sweet)
  chocolate, chopped coarsely
200g (6½ ounces) butter, chopped coarsely
3 eggs
3 egg yolks
⅓ cup (75g) caster (superfine) sugar
1 tablespoon cocoa powder

1 Preheat oven to 160°C/325°F. Grease
20cm x 30cm (8-inch x 12-inch) rectangular
pan; line base and long sides with baking paper,
extending paper 5cm (2 inches) over sides.
2 Place biscuits in a single layer over base of
pan, trimming to fit if necessary.
3 Combine chocolate and butter in medium
saucepan; stir over low heat until smooth.
Remove from heat.
4 Beat eggs, egg yolks and sugar in medium
bowl with electric mixer until thick and creamy;
beat in warm chocolate mixture.
5 Pour mixture over biscuits. Bake about 25
minutes or until filling is set. Cool 15 minutes
then refrigerate 1 hour. Dust slice with sifted
cocoa before cutting.

tip **Store slice in an airtight container in the fridge for up
to four days.**

DATE AND APPLE MUESLI SLICE

prep + cook time **45 minutes** makes **32**

2 medium apples (300g), grated coarsely
2 tablespoons lemon juice
¼ cup (60ml) water
50g (1½ ounces) butter
2 cups (340g) seeded dried dates
2 cups (220g) toasted muesli
1 cup (220g) firmly packed light brown sugar
1 cup (150g) plain all-purpose flour
1 teaspoon ground cinnamon

date and apple muesli slice

1 Preheat oven to 180°C/350°F. Grease
23cm x 32cm (9-inch x 13-inch) swiss roll pan;
line base with baking paper, extending paper
5cm (2 inches) over long sides.
2 Combine apple, juice, the water, butter
and dates in medium saucepan; bring to the
boil. Reduce heat; simmer, covered, about
5 minutes or until apple is soft. Uncover; cook,
stirring occasionally, about 5 minutes or until
mixture thickens to a paste-like consistency.
3 Meanwhile, combine muesli, sugar, flour and
cinnamon in large bowl.
4 Stir date mixture into muesli mixture; spread
mixture into pan; bake about 20 minutes or
until firm. Cool slice in pan before cutting.

tip **Store slice in an airtight container for up to three days.**

NO-BAKE CHOCOLATE SLICE

prep + cook time **25 minutes (+ refrigeration)** makes **24**

200g (6½ ounces) white marshmallows
1 tablespoon water
90g (3 ounces) butter, chopped coarsely
200g (6½ ounces) dark eating (semi-sweet)
  chocolate, chopped coarsely
125g (4 ounces) plain sweet biscuits,
  chopped coarsely
½ cup (125g) halved glacé cherries
½ cup (75g) roasted hazelnuts
½ cup (50g) walnuts
200g (6½ ounces) dark eating (semi-sweet)
  chocolate, melted, extra
60g (2 ounces) butter, melted, extra

1 Grease two 8cm x 25cm (3½-inch x 10-inch) bar pans; line bases with baking paper, extending paper 5cm (2 inches) over long sides.
2 Stir marshmallows, the water and butter in medium saucepan over low heat until marshmallows are melted. Remove from heat; stir in chocolate until smooth. Stir in biscuits, cherries and nuts.
3 Spread mixture evenly between pans (do not crush biscuits). Cover; refrigerate 1 hour.
4 Combine extra chocolate and extra butter; spread mixture evenly over slices. Refrigerate 1 hour or until firm.

tips **Store slice in an airtight container, in the fridge, for up to a week. Pecans can be used instead of walnuts.**

cashew ginger squares

CASHEW GINGER SQUARES

prep + cook time **40 minutes** makes **30**

125g (4 ounces) butter, softened
¼ cup (55g) caster (superfine) sugar
1 cup (150g) self-raising flour
1 teaspoon ground ginger
topping
½ cup (80g) icing (confectioners') sugar
60g (2 ounces) butter
2 tablespoons golden syrup or treacle
1 cup (150g) roasted unsalted cashews,
    chopped coarsely
¼ cup (50g) finely chopped glacé ginger

1 Preheat oven to 180°C/350°F. Grease 20cm x 30cm (8-inch x 12-inch) rectangular pan; line base with baking paper, extending paper 5cm (2 inches) over long sides.
2 Beat butter and sugar in small bowl with electric mixer until light and fluffy; stir in sifted flour and ginger. Spread mixture over base of pan.
3 Bake base about 20 minutes or until browned lightly; cool in pan.
4 Meanwhile, make topping; spread hot topping over cold base. Cool slice in pan before cutting.

topping Stir sifted icing sugar, butter and syrup in small saucepan over heat until butter is melted. Stir in nuts and ginger.

tip **Store slice in an airtight container, in the fridge, for up to a week.**

PEPITA AND SESAME SLICE

prep + cook time **40 minutes** makes **16**

90g (3 ounces) butter, softened
1 teaspoon grated lemon rind
2 tablespoons caster (superfine) sugar
1 egg
⅔ cup (100g) white plain (all-purpose) flour
½ cup (80g) wholemeal plain
  (all-purpose) flour
½ cup (80g) unsalted pepitas,
  chopped coarsely
¼ cup (80g) apricot jam
2 tablespoons sesame seeds, toasted

1 Preheat oven to 200°C/400°F. Grease 22cm (9-inch) square slab pan; line base with baking paper, extending paper 5cm (2 inches) over two opposite sides.
2 Beat butter, rind, sugar and egg in small bowl with electric mixer until light and fluffy. Stir in sifted flours and pepitas. Press mixture evenly into pan. Spread slice with jam; sprinkle with seeds.
3 Bake slice about 20 minutes or until browned lightly. Cool slice in pan before cutting.
tip **Store slice in an airtight container for up to a week.**

CHOCOLATE PEPPERMINT SLICE

prep + cook time **20 minutes (+ refrigeration)** makes **24**

250g (8 ounces) plain sweet biscuits
100g (3 ounces) butter, chopped coarsely
½ cup (125ml) sweetened condensed milk
70g (2½ ounces) peppermint crisp chocolate
    bars, chopped coarsely
chocolate topping
200g (6½ ounces) milk eating chocolate,
    chopped coarsely
2 teaspoons vegetable oil

1 Grease 19cm x 29cm (7½-inch x 11½-inch)
slice pan; line base with baking paper, extending
paper 5cm (2 inches) over long sides.
2 Process 200g (6½ ounces) of the biscuits
until fine. Chop remaining biscuits coarsely.
3 Combine butter and condensed milk in
small saucepan; stir over low heat until smooth.
Combine processed and chopped biscuits with
chocolate bar in medium bowl; stir in butter
mixture. Press mixture firmly into pan;
refrigerate about 20 minutes or until set.
4 Meanwhile, stir ingredients for chocolate
topping in small heatproof bowl over small
saucepan of simmering water, until smooth;
spread mixture over slice. Refrigerate until firm
before cutting.
tip **Store slice in an airtight container for up to a week.**

variations

lemon Replace peppermint crisp bars with
1 teaspoon finely grated lemon rind and
1 tablespoon lemon juice in the biscuit mixture.
Press mixture firmly into pan; refrigerate about
20 minutes or until set. Top with lemon icing
made by stirring 1¼ cups (200g) icing
(confectioners') sugar with 10g (½ ounce)
butter and one tablespoon lemon juice in small
heatproof bowl over small saucepan of
simmering water until smooth.

apricot & coconut Replace peppermint
crisp bars with ½ cup (40g) toasted shredded
coconut and ½ cup (80g) finely chopped dried
apricots in the biscuit mixture. Press mixture
firmly into pan; refrigerate about 20 minutes
or until set. Top with icing made by stirring
200g (6½ ounces) coarsely chopped white
eating chocolate and 2 teaspoons vegetable
oil in small heatproof bowl over small saucepan
of simmering water until smooth.

coffee & macadamia Replace peppermint
crisp bars with ½ cup (70g) coarsely chopped
roasted macadamias in the biscuit mixture.
Press mixture firmly into pan; refrigerate about
20 minutes or until set. Top with icing made by
dissolving 2 teaspoons instant coffee granules
in 2 tablespoons boiling water in small
heatproof bowl over small saucepan of
simmering water; add 1¼ cups (200g) icing
(confectioners') sugar and 10g (½ ounce)
butter, stirring until smooth.

CHOCOLATE RUM AND RAISIN SLICE

prep + cook time **55 minutes** makes **32**

125g (4 ounces) butter, chopped coarsely
200g (6½ ounces) dark eating (semi-sweet)
  chocolate, chopped coarsely
½ cup (110g) caster (superfine) sugar
1 cup (170g) coarsely chopped raisins
2 eggs, beaten lightly
1½ cups (225g) plain (all-purpose) flour
1 tablespoon dark rum

1 Preheat oven to 160°C/325°F. Grease
20cm x 30cm (8-inch x 12-inch) rectangular pan.
2 Stir butter, chocolate, sugar and raisins in
medium saucepan over low heat until
chocolate is melted. Cool to room temperature.
3 Stir remaining ingredients into chocolate
mixture; spread mixture into pan.
4 Bake about 30 minutes; cool slice in pan
before cutting.

tip Store slice in an airtight container for up to three
days. Rum has a very distinctive taste: we like to use
an underproof rum, but, if you like, use the stronger
overproof variety.

fruity white chocolate slice

HONEY AND COCONUT MUESLI SLICE

prep + cook time **50 minutes** makes **36**

2½ cups (225g) rolled oats
1 cup (35g) rice bubbles
½ cup (40g) shredded coconut
½ cup (70g) slivered almonds
1 tablespoon honey
395g (14 ounces) canned
    sweetened condensed milk

1 Preheat oven to 160°C/325°F. Grease 23cm x 32cm (9-inch x 13-inch) swiss roll pan; line base with baking paper, extending paper 5cm (2 inches) over long sides.
2 Combine oats, rice bubbles, coconut, nuts, honey and condensed milk in large bowl; press mixture firmly into pan. Bake about 40 minutes or until browned lightly. Cool slice in pan before cutting.

tip Store slice in an airtight container for up to a week.

FRUITY WHITE CHOCOLATE SLICE

prep + cook time **1 hour** makes **24**

⅔ cup (90g) slivered almonds
1¼ cups (210g) brazil nuts, chopped coarsely
1½ cups (135g) desiccated coconut
1 cup (150g) finely chopped dried apricots
1 cup (150g) dried currants
¼ cup (35g) plain (all-purpose) flour
1⅔ cup (250g) white chocolate melts, melted
½ cup (160g) apricot jam, warmed, strained
½ cup (180g) honey

1 Preheat oven to 160°C/325°F. Grease 19cm x 29cm (7½-inch x 11½-inch) slice pan; line base with baking paper, extending paper 5cm (2 inches) over long sides.
2 Combine nuts, coconut, dried fruit and flour in large bowl. Stir in combined hot melted chocolate, jam and honey; spread mixture into pan.
3 Bake about 45 minutes; cool slice in pan before cutting.

tip Store slice in an airtight container in the fridge for up to a week.

honey and coconut muesli slice

choc peanut butter squares

CHOC PEANUT BUTTER SQUARES

prep + cook time **25 minutes** (+ refrigeration) makes **36**

¾ cup (210g) smooth peanut butter
50g (1½ ounces) unsalted butter, softened
¼ cup (55g) firmly packed dark brown sugar
1 cup (160g) icing (confectioners') sugar
250g (8 ounces) milk eating chocolate,
   chopped coarsely
¼ cup (35g) roasted crushed peanuts

1 Preheat oven to 180°C/350°F. Grease deep
20cm (8-inch) square loose-based cake pan.
2 Combine peanut butter, butter, brown
sugar and sifted icing sugar in medium
bowl; press mixture evenly over base of pan.
Bake 10 minutes.
3 Meanwhile, combine chocolate and nuts
in small saucepan; stir over low heat until
chocolate is melted, pour over base.
Refrigerate 3 hours or overnight until set.

tips **Store squares in an airtight container for up to three
days; they taste better at room temperature than if eaten
cold from the refrigerator.**

no-bowl chocolate nut slice

NO-BOWL CHOCOLATE NUT SLICE

prep + cook time **40 minutes** makes **18**

90g (3 ounces) butter, melted
1 cup (100g) plain sweet biscuit crumbs
1½ cups (285g) dark choc bits
1 cup (70g) shredded coconut
1 cup (140g) crushed mixed nuts
395g (12½ ounces) canned sweetened
   condensed milk

1 Preheat oven to 180°C/350°F. Grease 22cm
(9-inch) square slab pan; line base with baking
paper, extending paper 5cm (2 inches) over
two opposite sides.
2 Pour butter into pan; sprinkle evenly with
biscuit crumbs, choc bits, coconut and nuts.
Drizzle with condensed milk.
3 Bake about 30 minutes; cool slice in pan
before cutting.

tip **Store slice in an airtight container, in the fridge, for
up to a week.**

LIME AND COCONUT SLICE

prep + cook time 25 minutes (+ refrigeration) makes 24

250g (8 ounces) plain sweet biscuits
1 teaspoon finely grated lime rind
1 tablespoon lime juice
½ cup (40g) shredded coconut
½ cup (125ml) sweetened condensed milk
90g (3 ounces) unsalted butter,
    chopped coarsely
lime icing
2 cups (320g) icing (confectioners') sugar
15g (½ ounce) unsalted butter, melted
2 tablespoons lime juice
1 tablespoon water, approximately

1 Grease 20cm x 30cm (8-inch x 12-inch) rectangular pan; line base with baking paper, extending paper 5cm (2 inches) over long sides.
2 Process 185g (6 ounces) of the biscuits until fine. Chop remaining biscuits coarsely. Combine processed and chopped biscuits, rind, juice and coconut in medium bowl.
3 Combine condensed milk and chopped butter in small saucepan; stir over medium heat until smooth. Add condensed milk mixture to biscuit mixture; stir to combine. Press mixture firmly into pan. Refrigerate 30 minutes or until firm.
4 Meanwhile, make lime icing.
5 Spread icing over slice. Refrigerate 30 minutes or until firm.
lime icing Sift icing sugar into small heatproof bowl; stir in butter, juice and enough water to make a thick paste. Place bowl over small saucepan of simmering water, stir until icing is spreadable.
tip Store slice in an airtight container for up to a week.

APRICOT CHOC-AROON SLICE

prep + cook time **1 hour (+ cooling)** makes **30**

Preheat oven to 150°C/300°F. Grease
20cm x 30cm (8-inch x 12-inch) rectangular
pan; line base and sides with baking paper,
extending paper 5cm (2 inches) over long
sides. Beat 3 egg whites in small bowl with
electric mixer until soft peaks form; gradually
add ½ cup (110g) caster (superfine) sugar,
beating until sugar dissolves. Fold in ¼ cup
(35g) plain (all-purpose) flour, 1⅓ cups (105g)
shredded coconut, ½ cup (80g) finely chopped
dried apricots and 90g (3 ounces) coarsely
grated milk eating chocolate. Spread mixture
into pan; bake 15 minutes. Sprinkle slice with ½
cup (70g) slivered almonds, press down gently;
bake about 30 minutes or until browned lightly.
Cool in pan. Drizzle with 90g (3 ounces) melted
milk eating chocolate; stand at room temperature
until set.

tip **Store slice in an airtight container for up to three days.**

CHOCOLATE BROWNIE SLICE

prep + cook time **1 hour** makes **25**

Preheat oven to 180°C/350°F. Grease deep
20cm (8-inch) square cake pan; line base with
baking paper, extending paper 5cm (2 inches)
over sides. Combine 125g (4 ounces) chopped
butter and 185g (6 ounces) chopped dark
eating (semi-sweet) chocolate in medium
saucepan; stir over low heat until smooth. Cool
10 minutes. Stir in ½ cup (110g) caster
(superfine) sugar and 2 eggs then 1¼ cups
sifted plain (all-purpose) flour, 155g (5 ounces)
chopped white eating chocolate and 90g
(3 ounces) chopped milk eating chocolate.
Spread mixture into pan. Bake about
35 minutes. Cool in pan.

tip **Store slice in an airtight container in the fridge for up
to four days.**

EASY ONE-BOWL SLICES

HEDGEHOG SLICE

prep + cook time **20 minutes (+ refrigeration)** makes **20**

Grease 20cm x 30cm (8-inch x 12-inch) rectangular pan; line base with baking paper, extending paper 5cm (2 inches) over long sides. Combine 395g (14 ounces) canned sweetened condensed milk and 90g (3 ounces) chopped unsalted butter in medium saucepan; stir over medium heat until smooth. Remove from heat; add 185g (6 ounces) chopped dark eating (semi-sweet) chocolate, stir until smooth. Break 250g (8 ounces) plain sweet biscuits into small pieces; place in large bowl with ⅔ cup (90g) roasted hazelnuts and ⅔ cup (110g) sultanas. Stir in chocolate mixture. Press mixture firmly into pan. Refrigerate 2 hours or until firm.

tips Store slice in an airtight container in the fridge for up to a week. We used plain sweet shortbread biscuits.

NUT AND CORN FLAKE SLICE

prep + cook time **30 minutes (+ refrigeration)** makes **24**

Grease 20cm x 30cm (8-inch x 12-inch) rectangular pan; line base with baking paper, extending paper 5cm (2 inches) over long sides. Stir 125g (4 ounces) coarsely chopped butter, ½ cup caster (superfine) sugar, ⅓ cup (80ml) light corn syrup and ⅓ cup (95g) crunchy peanut butter in large saucepan over low heat until sugar dissolves. Bring to the boil. Reduce heat; simmer, uncovered, without stirring, 5 minutes. Gently stir in 4 cups (160g) corn flakes. Spread mixture into pan; press firmly. Refrigerate about 30 minutes or until set. Spread 350g (11 ounces) milk eating chocolate over slice; stand at room temperature until set.

tip Store slice in an airtight container for up to three days.

BUTTER CREAM

Beat 125g (4 ounces) softened butter in small bowl with electric mixer until as white as possible; beat in 1½ cups (240g) sifted icing (confectioners') sugar and 2 tablespoons milk, in two batches.

makes 1¾ cups

tips Add any flavoured essence or extract you like to the butter cream. Beat it with the butter for the best flavour. Any citrus rind can be added. Beat 2 teaspoons finely grated rind with the butter and use juice of the fruit instead of milk. Butter cream is the most popular frosting, it's easy to spread and handle. Be aware that it's cream in colour, so added colouring will result in the colour being slightly yellow, particularly pinks and reds.

DARK CHOCOLATE GANACHE

Bring ½ cup (125ml) pouring cream to the boil in small saucepan; remove from heat. When bubbles subside, add 200g (6½ ounces) coarsely chopped dark eating (semi-sweet) chocolate; stir until smooth.

makes 1 cup

tips The ganache can be used while still warm and pourable, or it can be beaten with a wooden spoon until spreadable. If you want the ganache lighter and fluffier, beat the cooled mixture in a bowl with an electric mixer.

milk chocolate Replace dark eating chocolate with same amount coarsely chopped milk eating chocolate.

white chocolate Replace the dark chocolate with 360g (11½ ounces) coarsely chopped white eating chocolate.

FLUFFY MOCK CREAM

Combine 2 tablespoons milk, ⅓ cup (80ml) water and 1 cup (220g) caster (superfine) sugar in small saucepan; stir over low heat, without boiling, until sugar is dissolved. Sprinkle 1 teaspoon gelatine over extra 2 tablespoons water in cup, add to pan; stir syrup until gelatine is dissolved. Cool to room temperature. Beat 250g (8 ounces) softened butter and ½ teaspoon vanilla extract in small bowl with electric mixer until as white as possible. While motor is operating, gradually pour in cold syrup; beat until light and fluffy. Mixture will thicken on standing.

makes 2 cups

tips This frosting is whiter, lighter and fluffier than butter cream, and colours better, too. Use any extract or essence you like to flavour the frosting.

FLUFFY FROSTING

Combine 1 cup (220g) caster (superfine) sugar and ⅓ cup (80ml) water in small saucepan; stir over heat, without boiling, until sugar is dissolved. Boil, uncovered, without stirring, about 5 minutes or until syrup reaches 116°C/235°F on a candy thermometer. Syrup should be thick but not coloured. Remove from heat, allow bubbles to subside. Beat 2 egg whites in small bowl with electric mixer until soft peaks form. While motor is operating, add hot syrup in a thin stream; beat on high speed about 10 minutes or until mixture is thick.

makes 2½ cups

tip If you don't have a candy thermometer, boil the syrup until it's thick with heavy bubbles, but not coloured. Remove from heat, let bubbles subside, then reassess the thickness of the syrup.

FROSTINGS, ICINGS & FILLINGS

ROYAL ICING

Sift 1½ cups (240g) icing (confectioners') sugar through a very fine sieve. Lightly beat 1 egg white in small bowl with an electric mixer; add icing sugar, one tablespoon at a time. When icing reaches firm peaks, use a wooden spoon to beat in ½ teaspoon lemon juice; cover tightly with plastic wrap.

makes **1 cup**

tip **Royal icing begins to set as soon as it's exposed to the air, so keep the icing covered tightly with plastic wrap while you're not working with it. Stir in a few drops of food colouring if required by the recipe.**

CREAM CHEESE FROSTING

Beat 30g (1 ounce) softened butter and 80g (2½ ounces) softened cream cheese in small bowl with electric mixer until light and fluffy; gradually beat in 1½ cups (240g) sifted icing (confectioners') sugar.

makes **1¼ cups**

tips **For a citrus flavour, beat 2 teaspoons finely grated orange, lemon or lime rind with the butter and cream cheese. This frosting goes particularly well with carrot and banana cakes. Like butter cream, it is very user-friendly, but it takes colourings slightly better than butter cream.**

DAIRY-FREE CHOCOLATE FROSTING

Combine 50g (1½ ounces) dairy-free spread, 2 tablespoons water and ¼ cup caster (superfine) sugar in small saucepan; stir over low heat until sugar dissolves. Combine ¾ cup (120g) sifted pure icing (confectioners') sugar and 2 tablespoons cocoa powder in medium bowl; gradually stir in hot spread mixture until smooth. Cover; refrigerate 20 minutes. Using a wooden spoon, beat frosting until spreadable.

makes **¾ cup**

tip **This frosting is easy to handle, rich and luscious, and perfect for people who can't tolerate dairy products. It's a good substitute for ganache.**

GLACE ICING

Sift 2 cups (320g) icing (confectioners') sugar into small heatproof bowl; stir in 1 teaspoon butter and enough hot water (approximately 2 tablespoons) to make a thick paste. Place bowl over small saucepan of simmering water; stir until icing is spreadable.

makes **1 cup**

tips **It's important that the icing only be warm, not hot, while it's being stirred over the pan of water – it will crystallise if over-heated.**

chocolate **Sift 2 teaspoons cocoa powder with the sugar and add as per the recipe.**

coffee **Dissolve 1 teaspoon instant coffee granules in the water.**

passionfruit **Stir in 1 tablespoon passionfruit pulp.**

ALLSPICE also called pimento or jamaican pepper; tastes like a combination of nutmeg, cumin, clove and cinnamon. Available whole or ground.

ALMONDS flat, pointy-tipped nuts having a pitted brown shell enclosing a creamy white kernel which is covered by a brown skin.

blanched brown skins removed.

meal also known as ground almonds.

slivered small pieces of almond cut lengthways.

BAKING PAPER also known as parchment paper or baking parchment; a silicone-coated paper that is primarily used for lining baking pans and oven trays so cakes and biscuits won't stick, making removal easy.

BICARBONATE OF SODA raising agent also known as baking soda.

BISCUITS also known as cookies.

chocolate an uniced, plain, hard chocolate biscuit.

sweet any plain sweet biscuit (or cookie) can be used.

BRAZIL NUT a South American tree and also the name of the tree's commercially harvested edible seed. Because of its high polyunsaturated fat content the shelled nut can quickly become rancid.

BUTTER we use salted butter unless stated otherwise; 125g is equal to 1 stick (4 ounces).

CASHEWS plump, kidney-shaped, golden-brown nuts with a distinctive sweet, buttery flavour and containing about 48 per cent fat. Because of this high fat content, they should be kept, sealed tightly, under refrigeration to avoid becoming rancid. We use roasted

unsalted cashews in this book, unless otherwise stated; they're available from health-food stores and most supermarkets. Roasting cashews brings out their intense nutty flavour.

CHOCOLATE

choc bits also known as chocolate chips or chocolate morsels; available in milk, white and dark chocolate. Made of cocoa liquor, cocoa butter, sugar and an emulsifier, these hold their shape in baking and are ideal for decorating.

dark eating also known as semi-sweet or luxury chocolate; made of a high percentage of cocoa liquor and cocoa butter, and little added sugar. Unless stated otherwise, we use dark eating chocolate in this book as it's ideal for use in desserts and cakes.

melts small discs of compounded milk, white or dark chocolate ideal for melting and moulding.

milk most popular eating chocolate, mild and very sweet; similar in make-up to dark chocolate with the difference being the addition of milk solids.

white contains no cocoa solids but derives its sweet flavour from cocoa butter. Very sensitive to heat.

CHOCOLATE HAZELNUT SPREAD also known as Nutella; made of cocoa powder, hazelnuts, sugar and milk.

CHOKITO BAR chocolate-coated caramel fudge bar that contains crunchy rice crisps.

CINNAMON available both in the piece (called sticks or quills) and ground into powder; one of the world's most common spices, used universally as a sweet, fragrant

flavouring for both sweet and savoury foods. The dried inner bark of the shoots of the Sri Lankan native cinnamon tree; much of what is sold as the real thing is in fact cassia, chinese cinnamon, from the bark of the cassia tree. Less expensive to process than true cinnamon, it is often blended with sri lankan cinnamon to produce the type of "cinnamon" most commonly found in supermarkets.

COCONUT

cream obtained commercially from the first pressing of the coconut flesh alone, without the addition of water; the second pressing (less rich) is sold as coconut milk. Available in cans and cartons at most supermarkets.

desiccated concentrated, dried, unsweetened and finely shredded coconut flesh.

extract synthetically produced from flavouring, oil and alcohol.

flaked dried flaked coconut flesh.

milk not the liquid found inside the fruit, which is called coconut water, but the diluted liquid from the second pressing of the white flesh of a mature coconut (the first pressing produces coconut cream). Available in cans and cartons at most supermarkets.

shredded unsweetened thin strips of dried coconut flesh.

COCOA POWDER also known as unsweetened cocoa; cocoa beans (cacao seeds) that have been fermented, roasted, shelled, ground into powder then cleared of most of the fat content.

CORN FLAKES commercially manufactured cereal made of dehydrated then baked crisp flakes of corn.

GLOSSARY

CORNFLOUR also known as cornstarch. Available made from corn or wheat (wheaten cornflour gives a lighter texture in cakes); often used as a thickening agent in cooking.

CRANBERRIES available dried and frozen; the berries have a rich, astringent flavour and can be used in cooking sweet and savoury dishes. The dried version can usually be substituted with other dried fruit.

CREAM we used fresh cream, also known as pure or pouring cream unless otherwise stated. Has no additves. Minimum fat content 35%.

sour a thick, commercially cultured sour cream with a minimum fat content of 35%; light sour cream has 18.5% fat.

thick (double) a dolloping cream with a minimum fat content of 45%.

thickened (heavy) a whipping cream containing thickener. Minimum fat content 35%.

CREAM CHEESE commonly called philadelphia or philly; a soft cow-milk cheese, its fat content ranges from 14 to 33 per cent.

DRIED CURRANTS tiny, almost black raisins so-named after a grape variety that originated in Corinth, Greece.

EGGS we use large chicken eggs weighing an average of 60g unless stated otherwise in the recipes in this book. If a recipe calls for raw or barely cooked eggs, exercise caution if there is a salmonella problem in your area, particularly in food eaten by children and pregnant women.

ESSENCE an essence is either a distilled concentration of a food quality or an artificial creation of it.

EXTRACT is made by actually extracting the flavour from a food product. In the case of vanilla, pods are soaked, usually in alcohol, to capture the authentic flavour.

FLOUR

cornflour see cornflour

plain also known as all-purpose; unbleached wheat flour is the best for baking: the gluten content ensures a strong dough, which produces a light result.

rice very fine, almost powdery, gluten-free flour; made from ground white rice. Used in baking, as a thickener, and in some Asian noodles and desserts.

self-raising all-purpose plain or wholemeal flour with baking powder and salt added; make yourself with plain or wholemeal flour sifted with baking powder in the proportion of 1 cup flour to 2 teaspoons baking powder.

wholemeal also known as wholewheat flour; milled with the wheat germ so is higher in fibre and more nutritional than plain flour.

FRECKLES chocolate discs covered with a liberal sprinkling of hundreds and thousands.

GELATINE we use dried (powdered) gelatine in this book; it's also available in sheet form known as leaf gelatine. A thickening agent made from either collagen, a protein found in animal connective tissue and bones, or certain algae (agar-agar). Three teaspoons of dried gelatine (8g or one sachet) is about the same as four gelatine leaves. The two types are interchangable but leaf gelatine gives a much clearer mixture than dried gelatine; it's perfect in dishes where appearance matters.

GINGER

glacé fresh ginger root preserved in sugar syrup. Crystallised ginger can be substituted if rinsed with warm water and dried before using.

ground also known as powdered ginger; used as a flavouring in cakes, pies and puddings but generally cannot be substituted for fresh ginger.

GLACÉ CHERRIES also called candied cherries; boiled in heavy sugar syrup and then dried.

GOLDEN SYRUP A by-product of refined sugarcane; pure maple syrup or honey can be substituted. Golden syrup and treacle (a thicker, darker syrup not unlike molasses), also known as flavour syrups, are similar sugar products made by partly breaking down sugar into its component parts and adding water

HAZELNUTS also known as filberts; plump, grape-sized, rich, sweet nut having a brown skin that is removed by rubbing heated nuts together vigorously in a tea-towel.

HONEY the variety sold in a squeezable container is not suitable for the recipes in this book.

JAM also known as preserve or conserve; most often made from fruit and sugar.

LIGHT CORN SYRUP an imported product available in some supermarkets, delicatessens and health food stores. Made from cornstarch, it is a popular ingredient in American cooking for frostings, jams and jellies.

MACADAMIAS native to Australia; fairly large, slightly soft, buttery rich nut. Used to make oil and macadamia butter; equally good in salads or cakes and pastries;

delicious eaten on their own. Should always be stored in the fridge to prevent their high oil content turning them rancid.

MAPLE SYRUP distilled from the sap of sugar maple trees found only in Canada and about ten states in the USA. Most often eaten with pancakes or waffles, but also used as an ingredient in baking or in preparing desserts. Maple-flavoured syrup is not an adequate substitute for the real thing.

MARMALADE a preserve, usually based on citrus fruit.

MARSHMALLOWS white and pastel-coloured sweets; made from sugar, glucose, gelatine and cornflour.

MIXED DRIED FRUIT a combination of sultanas, raisins, currants, mixed peel and cherries.

MIXED SPICE a classic spice mixture generally containing caraway, allspice, coriander, cumin, nutmeg and ginger, although cinnamon and other spices can be added. It is used with fruit and in cakes.

MUESLI also known as granola, a combination of grains (mainly oats), nuts and dried fruits. Some manufacturers toast their product in oil and honey, adding crispness and kilojoules.

PEANUT BUTTER peanuts ground to a paste; available in crunchy and smooth varieties.

PEANUTS also known as groundnut, not in fact a nut but the pod of a legume. We mainly use raw (unroasted) or unsalted roasted peanuts.

PECANS native to the US and now grown locally; pecans are golden brown, buttery and rich. Good in savoury as well as sweet dishes; walnuts are a good substitute.

PEPITAS are the pale green kernels of dried pumpkin seeds; they can be bought plain or salted.

PISTACHIOS green, delicately flavoured nuts inside hard off-white shells. Available salted or unsalted in their shells; you can also get them shelled.

PRUNES dried fruit made from commercially or sun-dried plums.

RAISINS dried sweet grapes (traditionally muscatel grapes).

RICE BUBBLES puffed rice product made with malt extract which contains gluten.

ROLLED OATS flattened oat grain rolled into flakes and traditionally used for porridge. Instant oats are also available, but use traditional oats for baking.

RUM we use a dark underproof rum (not overproof) for a more subtle flavour in cooking. White rum is almost colourless, sweet and used mostly in mixed drinks.

SESAME SEEDS black and white are the most common of this small oval seed, however there are also red and brown varieties. The seeds are used as an ingredient and as a condiment. Roast the seeds in a heavy-based frying pan over low heat to enhance the flavour.

SHERRY fortified wine consumed as an aperitif or used in cooking. Sold as fino (light, dry), amontillado (medium sweet, dark) and oloroso (full-bodied, very dark).

SUGAR we use coarse, granulated table sugar, also known as crystal sugar, unless otherwise specified.
brown a soft, finely granulated sugar retaining molasses for its characteristic colour and flavour.
caster also known as superfine or finely granulated table sugar.
demerara small-grained golden-coloured crystal sugar.
icing also known as confectioners' sugar or powdered sugar; pulverised granulated sugar crushed together with a small amount of cornflour.

SULTANAS also known as golden raisins; dried seedless white grapes used in fruit cakes and baking.

SWEETENED CONDENSED MILK a canned milk product consisting of milk with more than half the water content removed and sugar added to the remaining milk.

VANILLA
bean dried, long, thin pod from a tropical golden orchid; the minuscule black seeds inside the bean are used to impart a luscious vanilla flavour in baking and desserts. Place a whole bean in a jar of sugar to make the vanilla sugar often called for in recipes; the same bean can be used three or four times.
extract obtained from vanilla beans infused in water; a non-alcoholic version of essence.

WALNUTS as well as being a good source of fibre and healthy oils, nuts contain a range of vitamins, minerals and other beneficial plant components called phytochemicals. Every nut has a special make-up and walnuts contain the beneficial omega-3 fatty acids.

CONVERSION CHART

MEASURES

One Australian metric measuring cup holds approximately 250ml, one Australian metric tablespoon holds 20ml, one Australian metric teaspoon holds 5ml.

The difference between one country's measuring cups and another's is within a 2- or 3-teaspoon variance, and will not affect your cooking results. North America, New Zealand and the United Kingdom use a 15ml tablespoon. All cup and spoon measurements are level. The most accurate way of measuring dry ingredients is to weigh them. When measuring liquids, use a clear glass or plastic jug with metric markings.

We use large eggs with an average weight of 60g.

DRY MEASURES

METRIC	IMPERIAL
15g	½oz
30g	1oz
60g	2oz
90g	3oz
125g	4oz (¼lb)
155g	5oz
185g	6oz
220g	7oz
250g	8oz (½lb)
280g	9oz
315g	10oz
345g	11oz
375g	12oz (¾lb)
410g	13oz
440g	14oz
470g	15oz
500g	16oz (1lb)
750g	24oz (1½lb)
1kg	32oz (2lb)

LIQUID MEASURES

METRIC	IMPERIAL
30ml	1 fluid oz
60ml	2 fluid oz
100ml	3 fluid oz
125ml	4 fluid oz
150ml	5 fluid oz
190ml	6 fluid oz
250ml	8 fluid oz
300ml	10 fluid oz
500ml	16 fluid oz
600ml	20 fluid oz
1000ml (1 litre)	1¾ pints

LENGTH MEASURES

METRIC	IMPERIAL
3mm	⅛in
6mm	¼in
1cm	½in
2cm	¾in
2.5cm	1in
5cm	2in
6cm	2½in
8cm	3in
10cm	4in
13cm	5in
15cm	6in
18cm	7in
20cm	8in
22cm	9in
25cm	10in
28cm	11in
30cm	12in (1ft)

OVEN TEMPERATURES

These oven temperatures are only a guide for conventional ovens.
For fan-forced ovens, check the manufacturer's manual.

	°C (CELSIUS)	°F (FAHRENHEIT)
Very slow	120	250
Slow	150	275-300
Moderately slow	160	325
Moderate	180	350-375
Moderately hot	200	400
Hot	220	425-450
Very hot	240	475

The imperial measurements used in these recipes are approximate only. Measurements for cake pans are approximate only. Using same-shaped cake pans of a similar size should not affect the outcome of your baking. We measure the inside top of the cake pan to determine sizes.

A

almonds
  almond butter cake 12
  almond carrot cake 9
  almond crisps 36
anzac biscuits 32
apricot & coconut slice 60
apricot choc-aroon slice 70

B

biscuits
  almond crisps 36
  anzac 32
  caramel pecan macaroons 40
  chewy chocolate caramel
    cookies 28
  chocolate chip cookies 28
  chunky chocolate chip
    cookies 26
  coconut macaroons 31
  cream cheese, coconut
    and lime cookies 35
  crunchy muesli cookies 39
  dutch ginger 43
  easy kids' 46–7
  golden oaty carrot 32
  jam drops 36
  macadamia shortbread 43
  pecan choc-chunk
    cookies 40
  spiced treacle cookies 31
  traditional shortbread 35
butter cream 72
buttercake, cut & keep 4

C

cakes
  almond butter 12
  almond carrot 9
  chocolate banana 16
  chocolate fudge 20
  cut & keep buttercake 4
  economical boiled fruit 12
  maple pecan 23
  one-bowl sultana loaf 19
  orange 20
  pineapple coconut 19

pineapple sultana 6
pound 15
prune and choc-chip 10
quick-mix chocolate 15
upside-down pear
  and pistachio 6
cashew ginger squares 57
chocolate
  apricot choc-aroon slice 70
  chewy chocolate caramel
    cookies 28
  choc peanut butter
    squares 67
  chocolate banana cake 16
  chocolate brownie slice 70
  chocolate chip cookies 28
  chocolate freckle slice 48
  chocolate fudge cake 20
  chocolate curl cakes 25
  chocolate peppermint
    slice 60
  chocolate rum and
    raisin slice 63
  chunky chocolate chip
    cookies 26
  creamy choc frosting 16
  dairy-free frosting 73
  dark chocolate ganache 72
  glacé icing 73
  hedgehog slice 71
  icing 15
  milk chocolate ganache 72
  no-bake chocolate slice 54
  no-bowl chocolate
    nut slice 67
  pecan choc-chunk
    cookies 40
  quick-mix chocolate cake 15
  triple chocolate slice 53
coconut
  apricot & coconut slice 60
  cream cheese, coconut
    and lime cookies 35
  honey and coconut slice 64
  lime and coconut slice 68

macaroons 31
pineapple coconut cake 19
coffee & macadamia slice 60
coffee glacé icing 73
cookies, see biscuits
cream cheese, coconut and
  lime cookies 35
cream cheese frosting 9, 73
cupcakes
  chocolate curl cakes 25
  daisy cakes 24
  strawberry cream cakes 25
  sugared berry cakes 24
cut & keep buttercake 4

D

dairy-free chocolate
  frosting 73
daisy cakes 24
date and apple muesli slice 53
dutch ginger biscuits 43

F

florentine slice 50
fluffy frosting 72
fluffy mock cream 72
frosting, see also icing
  cream cheese 9, 73
  creamy choc 16
  dairy-free chocolate 73
  fluffy 72
fruit cake, economical boiled 12
fruity white chocolate slice 64

G

ganache
  dark chocolate 72
  milk chocolate 72
ginger
  cashew ginger squares 57
  dutch ginger biscuits 43
  ginger lime shortbreads 45

INDEX

glacé icing 73
  chocolate 73
  coffee 73
  passionfruit 73
golden oaty carrot biscuits 32
golden syrup peanut swirls 45

H
hedgehog slice 71
honey and coconut slice 64

I
icing, see also frosting
  chocolate 15
  chocolate glacé 73
  coffee glacé 73
  lime 68
  lime glacé 19
  passionfruit glacé 73
  royal 73

J
jam drops 36

K
kids' biscuits
  flowers 46
  hearts 46
  ribbons and bows 47
  rocket man 47

L
latte shortbread dippers 44
lemon slice 60
lemon squares, tangy 50
lime and coconut slice 68
lime glacé icing 19
lime icing 68

M
macadamia shortbread 43
macaroons
  caramel pecan 40
  coconut 31
maple butterscotch sauce 23
maple pecan cake 23
muesli cookies, crunchy 39
muesli slice, date and apple 53
muesli slice, honey
  and coconut 64

N
nuts
  almond butter cake 12
  almond carrot cake 9
  almond crisps 36
  caramel pecan macaroons 40
  cashew ginger squares 57
  choc peanut butter
    squares 67
  coffee & macadamia slice 60
  florentine slice 50
  ginger, lime and cashew
    shortbreads 45
  golden syrup peanut
    swirls 45
  hedgehog slice 71
  macadamia shortbread 43
  maple pecan cake 23
  no-bowl chocolate nut slice 67
  nut and corn
    flake slice 71
  pecan choc-chunk
    cookies 40
  upside-down pear and
    pistachio cake 6

O
one-bowl sultana loaf 19
orange cake 20

P
passionfruit glacé icing 73
pear and pistachio cake,
  upside-down 6
pecans
  caramel pecan
    macaroons 40
  maple pecan cake 23
  pecan choc-chunk
    cookies 40
pepita and sesame slice 58
pineapple coconut cake 19
pineapple sultana cake 6
pound cake 15
prune and choc-chip
  cake 10

R
royal icing 73

S
sauce, maple butterscotch 23
shortbread
  basic shortbread dough 44
  ginger lime shortbreads 45
  golden syrup peanut swirls 45
  latte shortbread dippers 44
  macadamia 43
  traditional 35
slices
  apricot & coconut 60
  apricot choc-aroon 70
  cashew ginger squares 57
  choc peanut butter
    squares 67
  chocolate brownie 70
  chocolate freckle 48
  chocolate peppermint 60
  chocolate rum and
    raisin 63
  coffee & macadamia 60
  date and apple muesli 53
  easy one-bowl 70
  florentine 50
  fruity white chocolate 64
  hedgehog 71
  honey and coconut 64
  lemon 60
  lime and coconut 68
  no-bake chocolate 54
  no-bowl chocolate nut 67
  nut and corn flake 71
  pepita and sesame 58
  tangy lemon squares 50
  triple chocolate 53
spiced treacle cookies 31
strawberry cream cakes 25
sugared berry cakes 24
sultana loaf, one-bowl 19

T
tangy lemon squares 50
treacle cookies, spiced 31

If you like this cookbook, you'll love these...